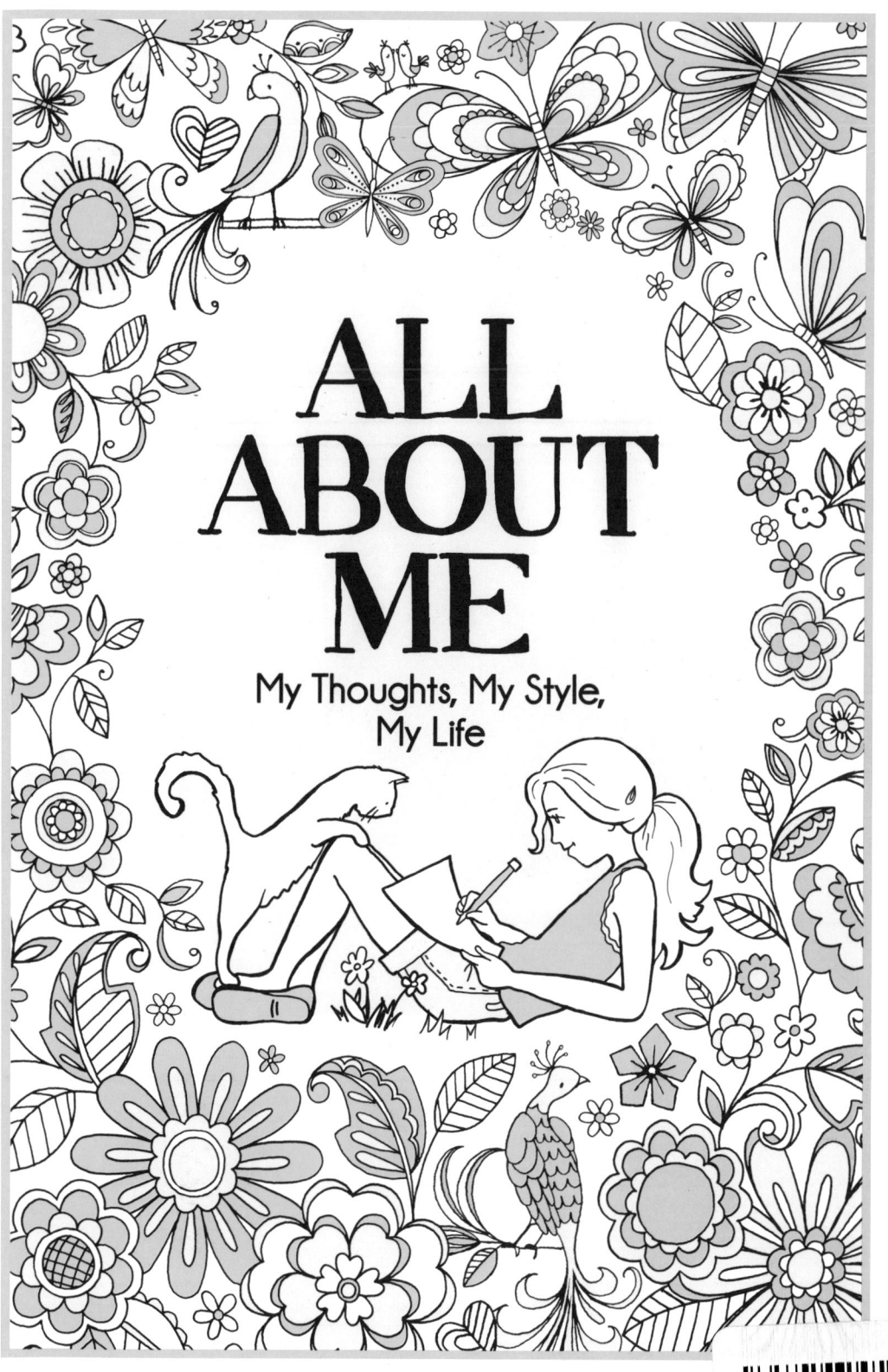

ALL ABOUT ME

My Thoughts, My Style,
My Life

WRITTEN BY ELLEN BAILEY

ILLUSTRATED BY NELLIE RYAN

EDITED BY LIZ SCOGGINS AND
JEN WAINWRIGHT
DESIGNED BY JACK CLUCAS
COVER ARTWORK BY BETH GUNNELL AND
KATY JACKSON
COVER DESIGNED BY ANGIE ALLISON

ALL ABOUT ME

My Thoughts, My Style, My Life

Buster Books

This edition first published in Great Britain in 2014 by Buster Books,
an imprint of Michael O'Mara Books Limited,
9 Lion Yard, Tremadoc Road, London SW4 7NQ

The material in this book was originally published in 2010
under the title *The Yearbook For Girls*

 www.busterbooks.co.uk

 Buster Children's Books

 @BusterBooks

A CIP catalogue record for this book is available from the British Library.

ISBN: 978-1-78055-138-8

4 6 8 10 9 7 5

This book was printed and bound in January 2016
by Shenzhen Wing King Tong Paper Products Co Ltd.,
Shenzhen, Guangdong, China.

Papers used by Buster Books are natural, recyclable products
made from wood grown in sustainable forests. The manufacturing processes
conform to the environmental regulations of the country of origin.

CONTENTS

GETTING STARTED

THIS BOOK IS ABOUT TO CHANGE YOUR LIFE. INSIDE, YOU WILL FIND TONS OF QUIZZES AND QUESTIONS THAT WILL MAKE YOU THINK AND MAKE YOU LAUGH. AS YOU FILL IN THE BLANK SPACES, YOU'LL MAKE A RECORD OF EXACTLY WHO YOU ARE THAT YOU CAN TREASURE FOREVER.

Here's how it works. You don't have to read this book in any particular order, as each section you fill in has a space to make a note of the date, time and place, like this:

Date .... Time .... Place ....

Each time there's a quiz or questionnaire, you'll need to fill out your opinion along the dotted line:

like this

or tick the box next to the answer you most agree with, like this:

☑ Yes ☐ No

aLL aBOUT Me:
THE FaCT FILE

Date .... Time .... Place ....

My name is ....

My nickname is ....

My birthday is on ....

I was born in the year ....

The place I was born is called ....

My star sign is ....

Right now I'm .... years old

I got this book on ....

My mum's name is ....

My dad's name is ....

I have .... brothers and .... sisters

Their names are ....

....

My school is called ....

My best friend is ....

I have .... pets

Signed ....

RIGHT HERE, RIGHT NOW

USE THIS PAGE TO MAKE A RECORD OF WHAT
YOU ARE DOING AT THIS EXACT MOMENT IN TIME.

Date ....

Time ....

Place ....

What sounds can you hear right now?

What are you wearing?

How have you done your hair?

Who are you with?

What is the weather like?

What can you see right now?

What's in your pocket?

Taking the measure

FILL IN YOUR ANSWERS BELOW, USING WHICHEVER UNITS OF MEASUREMENT YOU PREFER – FOR INSTANCE, YOU CAN MEASURE YOUR HEIGHT IN FEET AND INCHES OR IN METRES AND CENTIMETRES.

Date .... Time .... Place ....

How tall are you? ....

How tall would you like to be? ....

eyes

Most people say their eyes are blue, brown, green or hazel. However, if you take a close look in the mirror you'll see flecks of all sorts of other colours in your irises – the coloured parts of your eyes. Use a set of coloured pencils on the picture below to show how many colours you can really see.

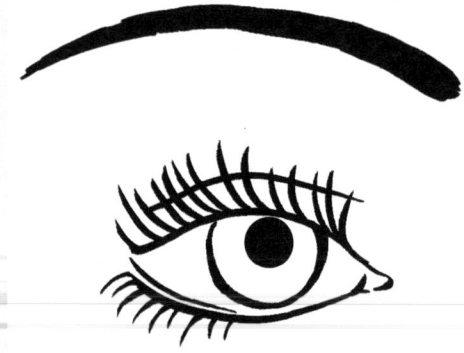

HANDS

Spread your fingers out as wide as they can go. What is the distance from the tip of your thumb to the tip of your little finger?

....

How long is your hand from the tip of your middle finger to the bottom of your palm?

....

What is the length of your little finger?

....

FEET

Are both your feet exactly the same length? ☐ Yes ☐ No

What colour would you most like to paint your toes? Use coloured pencils and make this foot look fancy.

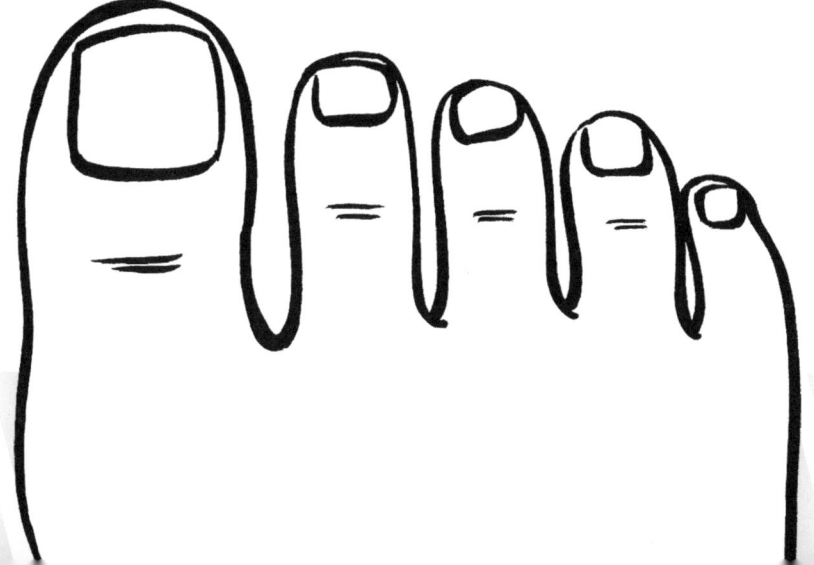

SUPERFAN OR SUPERSTAR?

STUDY EACH OF THE OPTIONS IN THE LIST BELOW AND TICK YOUR PREFERENCE. COUNT UP YOUR ANSWERS AND FIND OUT THE RESULTS – MORE HEARTS MEANS YOU'RE A SUPERFAN, MORE STARS AND YOU'RE A SUPERSTAR!

Date .... Time .... Place ....

Fish fingers	or	Oysters
Photographer	or	Model
Takeaway	or	Restaurant
Milk chocolate	or	Dark chocolate
Shower	or	Bubble bath
Trainers	or	High-heels
Autograph hunter	or	Autograph signer
Good friends	or	Entourage
Kitten	or	Lapdog
Minibus	or	Tour bus

LOOK TO THE FUTURE

Date ....

Time .... Place ....

In ten years' time I want to live in

.... with ....

My pet will be a .... called

.... I want to be able to

.... My greatest achievement

will be .... I will have met

.... in real life.

WHAT WILL BE, WILL BE

WHAT DO YOU THINK THE FUTURE WILL BE LIKE? WHAT THINGS DO YOU THINK WILL BE MORE POPULAR, AND WHAT DO YOU THINK WILL BE LESS POPULAR?

Date .... Time .... Place ....

Perhaps you think that recycling will be going up, and cars will be going down. Or maybe curly hair will be going up, and straight hair will be going down. Fill the arrows below with your predictions.

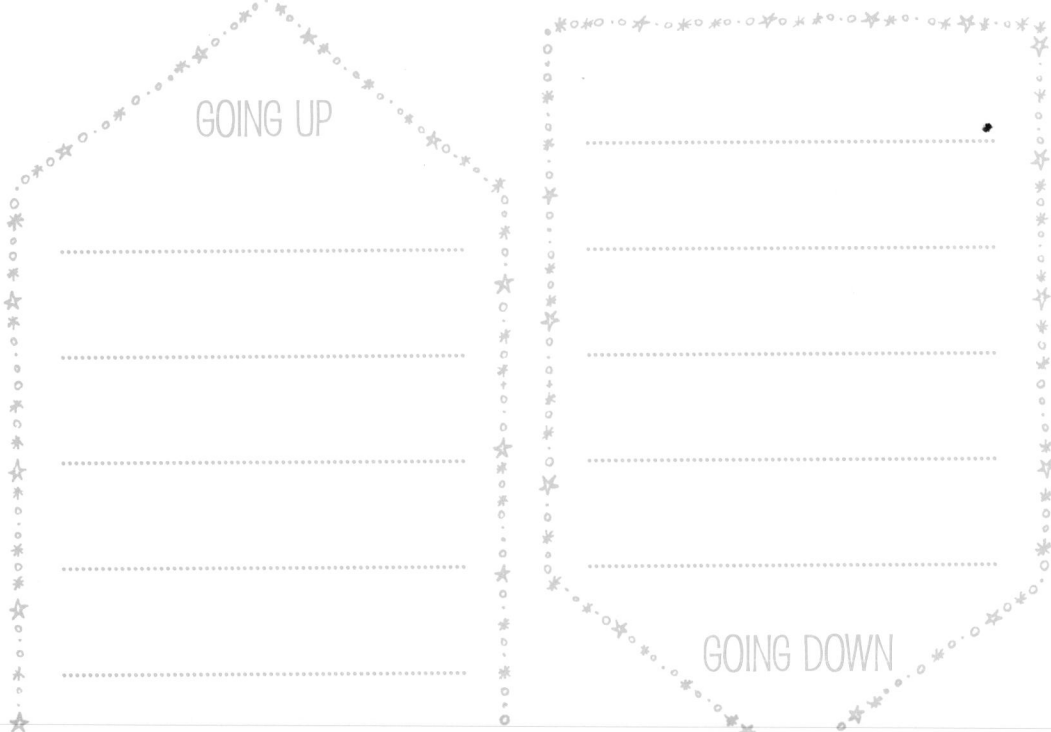

GOING UP

GOING DOWN

TEN THINGS TO ACHIEVE THIS YEAR

TRY TO ACHIEVE EACH OF THESE IDEAS WITHIN THE YEAR AND TICK EACH ONE OFF AS SOON AS YOU MANAGE IT.

Date .... Time .... Place ....

☐ Raise some money for charity

☐ Laugh so hard my sides hurt

☐ Master a recipe

☐ Make at least one completely new friend

☐ Visit a place I've never been to before

☐ Make someone a birthday present from scratch

☐ Perform something in public

☐ Overcome one of my fears

MOODY MOMENTS

USE THIS SECTION TO UNLOAD ANYTHING YOU LIKE. YOU'LL BE FEELING LIGHTER IN NO TIME.

Date .... Time .... Place ....

Is anything annoying you right now? ☐ Yes ☐ No

If 'yes', what is it? ....

Who did you last argue with? ....

What about? ....

Have you made up yet? ☐ Yes ☐ No

Are you worried about anything? ☐ Yes ☐ No

If 'yes', what is it? ....

What are you happiest about right now?

....

Mirror, Mirror

Date ....
Time ....
Place ....

DRAW A PICTURE OF YOURSELF IN THE MIRROR,
THEN WRITE THREE WORDS THAT DESCRIBE HOW
YOU'RE FEELING TODAY AROUND THE OUTSIDE.

TEN THINGS TO STOP WORRYING ABOUT THIS YEAR

MAKE A PROMISE TO YOURSELF THAT YOU'LL WORRY LESS THIS YEAR.
WRITE DOWN YOUR TEN BIGGEST WORRIES IN THE BALLOONS BELOW,
THEN WORK ON MAKING THEM FLOAT AWAY ...

Date   Time   Place

2.

1.

3.

4.

5.

7.

6.

8.

10.

9.

THAT'S SO ANNOYING

FIND THE THING THAT ANNOYS YOU MOST OF ALL IN THE WORLD.

Date   Time   Place

Write down four things that really annoy you in the first row, such as wasps or people kicking the back of your chair. Choose which thing from each pair is the most annoying, then decide which of the final two is the thing that annoys you most of all in the world.

all in a NIGHT'S SLEEP

COMPLETE THIS QUESTIONNAIRE TO RECORD YOUR SLEEPING HABITS.

Date .... Time .... Place ....

Do you share your bedroom? Yes ☐ No ☐

If 'yes', who with? ....

Blankets ☐ or Duvet ☐ ?

What colour is your bedding? ....

What time do you normally go to bed? ....

What do you wear to bed? ....

Have you ever:

Fallen out of bed? ☐
Woken up with your feet at the pillow end? ☐
Wriggled so much that your sheets came off in the night? ☐

SLEEP STYLE

THE POSITION YOU SLEEP IN COULD TELL YOU A LOT ABOUT YOUR PERSONALITY. LOOK AT THE PICTURE BELOW AND CIRCLE THE IMAGE THAT'S MOST LIKE YOU WHEN YOU FALL ASLEEP.

Date .... Time .... Place ....

'The Soldier'
position

'The Freefall'
position

'The Foetal'
position

What Your Sleep Style Means

If you sleep in 'The Soldier' position, lying flat on your back with your arms by your sides, you're a thoughtful and quiet person and you value your alone time. You're a perfectionist and you hate laziness. You always set very high expectations for yourself, but remember it's okay to relax and let your hair down sometimes.

If you're a 'Freefaller' at night time - sleeping on your front with your arms on or underneath your pillow and your head turned to one side - then you're a real social butterfly. You've got tons of friends and you love to stay active. You're an emotional person, but you occasionally need to learn to keep your temper in check.

People who sleep in 'The Foetal' position - lying on one side, slightly curled up and with their knees bent - are generous spirited with a big heart. If you sleep like this, you can be a real tough cookie, and hate people seeing you upset. You've got a close group of friends who you can lean on, though, so don't be afraid to let your emotions out.

sweet dreams

write down the most vivid dreams you've ever had in each of the clouds below.

Date ....

Time .... Place ....

FUNNIEST
THINGS OF ALL TIME

THINK OF THE TEN FUNNIEST THINGS THAT HAVE EVER HAPPENED TO YOU, OR THAT YOU'VE SEEN IN A FILM OR ON TV. ORGANIZE THEM WITH YOUR FAVOURITE AT NUMBER ONE.

Date .... Time .... Place ....

1. ....
2. ....
3. ....
4. ....
5. ....
6. ....
7. ....
8. ....
9. ....
10. ....

FASHION Favourites

TICK YOUR FAVOURITE STYLES IN EACH OF THE CATEGORIES BELOW. THEN DRAW YOUR DREAM OUTFIT ON THE MODEL. USE THE FRAMES AROUND THE MODEL TO DESCRIBE YOUR CREATION.

Date .... Time .... Place ....

Neckline: Halter ☐ V-neck ☐ Square ☐ Round ☐

Hat: Beret ☐ Baseball cap ☐ Straw hat ☐ Bobble hat ☐

Material: Silk ☐ Cotton ☐ Denim ☐ Wool ☐ Leather ☐

Shopping: High street ☐ Market ☐ Boutique ☐

Shoes: Flip-flops ☐ Trainers ☐ High-heels ☐ Pumps ☐

Bag: Clutch ☐ Backpack ☐ Basket ☐ Duffle ☐

Pattern: Swirly ☐ Flowery ☐ Animal ☐ Geometric ☐

Jeans: Skinny ☐ Flared ☐ Baggy ☐ Boot-cut ☐

Your look: Designer ☐ Vintage ☐ Home-made ☐

Your style: Urban ☐ Sporty ☐ Romantic ☐ Preppy ☐

WHAT'S YOUR STYLE?

TAKE THIS QUIZ TO FIND OUT MORE ABOUT YOURSELF AND YOUR STYLE.
FOR EACH CATEGORY, CIRCLE THE OPTION THAT BEST DESCRIBES YOU,
THEN CHECK OUT WHAT YOUR RESULTS MEAN ON PAGE 33.

Date   Time   Place

YOUR HAIR

a. Bold and trendy
b. Tied back off your face
c. Long and shiny
d. Short and spiky

YOUR DREAM JOB

a. Film star
b. Athlete
c. Fashion designer
d. Professor

YOUR LOOK

a. Bright and vibrant
b. Relaxed and sporty
c. Pretty and girly
d. Comfy and cosy

your perfect saturday

a. Karaoke

b. Go-karting

c. Shopping spree

d. Museum

homework ...

a. ... will always be perfectly presented

b. ... will be done as quickly as possible

c. ... can wait til later

d. ... needs time to be done properly.

your fave snack

a. An elaborate French pastry

b. Fresh fruit

c. A refreshing tropical drink

d. Cubes of stinky cheese

with your friends, you're ...

a. ... leader of the pack

b. ... mates with the whole team

c. ... one of the girls

d. ... best friends forever

your star skill

a. A great voice
b. Strength and speed
c. A passion for fashion
d. The biggest brains of them all

your Dream Holiday

a. Drama camp
b. An adventure holiday
c. A relaxing time by a pool
d. Sightseeing in a city

If you were a BOY for a Day, you'D ...

a. ... be lead singer in a rock band
b. ... join the rugby team
c. ... style your hair all day
d. ... spend the day studying.

your style answers

Mostly 'A's: Fun and flamboyant

You have plenty of confidence, and don't mind standing out from the crowd. You might surprise a lot of people with your softer side, so don't forget to let it show sometimes.

Mostly 'B's: Sporty miss

You have bags of energy and can't help but be outgoing. You love to try new things, and make friends easily. Don't forget to take a break every now and then, to give yourself the chance to relax.

Mostly 'C's: Party princess

You love to spend time on your appearance, and enjoy being pampered. That doesn't mean you don't have a serious side, and you'll often surprise your friends and family with your clever and witty observations.

Mostly 'D's: Ahead of the game.

You're very organized and usually like to make sure you're on top of things. Your parents and teachers probably appreciate how hard you study. Although you like to look before you leap, remember to save time to have fun with friends.

LOVE IT, HATE IT

COLOUR IN THE HEARTS BELOW. USE PINK IF YOU LOVE WHAT'S WRITTEN INSIDE THE HEART, BLUE IF YOU HATE IT, AND YELLOW IF YOU DON'T FEEL STRONGLY EITHER WAY.

Date .... Time .... Place ....

FILMS AT THE CINEMA

BOYS

CAMPING

HOROSCOPES

SHOPPING

BEING NEAT AND TIDY

KARAOKE

SPICY FOOD

CHATTING WITH FRIENDS

FAIRGROUND RIDES

SCHOLastic Fantastic

PEOPLE OFTEN SAY THAT SCHOOL DAYS ARE THE BEST DAYS OF
YOUR LIFE, BUT WHAT REALLY GOES ON AT YOUR SCHOOL?

Date .... Time .... Place ....

I love it at school when ....

I hate it at school when ....

My school uniform is

okay ☐   awful ☐   I don't have one ☐

The best school trip I've ever been on was to ....

....

My favourite subject is ....

My favourite teacher is ....

The funniest person in my class is ....

The cleverest person in my class is ....

I last got in trouble because I ....

....

....

My best excuse for being late is ....

....

I eat my lunch with ....

At break time, I like to ....

career day

answer these questions to discover your career destiny. as you go along, make a note of each time you answer a, b, c or d. then turn to page 41 for your results.

Date .... Time .... Place ....

From the following subjects, which is your favourite?

a. Art

b. P.E.

c. Drama

d. Science

Which of these holidays would you prefer?

a. Relaxing in a beautiful country cottage
b. Camping somewhere with stunning scenery
c. Staying at a hotel in a stylish, fast-paced city
d. Visiting amazing ancient buildings in distant locations

What are you most likely to be in charge of in a group project?

a. Drawing illustrations and creating charts
b. Presenting the project to the class at the end
c. Taking the lead and managing the project
d. Researching the project and providing the key facts

How would you help your best friend celebrate her birthday?

a. Invite a few of her very best friends round for a sleepover
b. Arrange a big picnic in the park
c. Invite everyone she knows to the party of the year
d. Take her to a show she's been talking about for ages

If you were an animal, which would you be?

a. A chimpanzee
b. A horse
c. A kitten
d. A lion

Which of the following would you most like to win?

a. The Nobel Peace Prize
b. A gold medal at the Olympics
c. Personality of the Year
d. The 'Women in Science' award

Which of these desserts would you most like to eat?

a. A big chocolate brownie
b. An ice lolly
c. A banana split
d. A strawberry tart

Which of the following gifts would you most like to receive?

a. A playlist put together by your best friend
b. A trip to a theme park
c. A new mobile phone
d. A computer game

Which of the following things is most important to you?

a. Creativity
b. Freedom
c. Happiness
d. Success.

career-Day answers

Mostly 'A's: People person

Thoughtful and creative - you'd make a brilliant interior designer, illustrator or novelist. Any career working with people would be ideal, too - perhaps as a teacher, a therapist or a carer.

Mostly 'B's: Outdoor girl

You love rolling up your sleeves to get stuck in. A job as a nature conservationist would be perfect, but you could also consider becoming a landscape gardener, a set designer or a journalist.

Mostly 'C's: Celeb-in-waiting

Of all the personality types, you're the most likely to become famous. You love to plan outings, so you'd be brilliant at public relations (organizing events such as book launches, restaurant openings, or press conferences). You could even work as a TV presenter or host your own radio show.

Mostly 'D's: High-flyer

You know your own mind and aren't afraid to study hard to make your dreams come true. You're destined for a career that makes lots of money and will earn you respect. A career as a doctor, architect, lawyer or banker would be perfect for you.

MOST
LIKELY TO ...

IT'S TIME TO NOMINATE YOUR FAVOURITE
PEOPLE FOR A SET OF VERY SPECIAL PRIZES.

Date ....
Time ....
Place ....

Do you have a friend who's always one step
ahead of the latest trend and is bound to
become a fashion icon? Or perhaps you
have a relative who loves to be the centre
of attention and is sure to end up on
television? In each of these frames, draw a
picture or glue a photo of the person you
think should receive the award written
above it. Don't forget to write the name
underneath each portrait.

WHO IS MOST LIKELY TO ...

... win a Nobel Prize?

... get detention?

... appear on TV?

... run a marathon?

... become a millionaire?

... break a bone?

... write a novel?

... work with animals?

... publish their memoirs?

... trip on the red carpet?

... become a fashion icon?

... raise their hand in class?

Free-Time Favourites

IF YOU HAD TO CHOOSE, HOW WOULD YOU MOST LIKE TO SPEND YOUR FREE TIME? PICK ONE OPTION FROM EACH ACTIVITY BELOW, THEN UNDERLINE YOUR ABSOLUTE-FAVOURITE ACTIVITY OF THEM ALL.

Date .... Time .... Place ....

Movies: Comedy ☐ Action ☐ Romance ☐ Scary ☐

Music: Pop ☐ Rock ☐ R&B ☐ Classical ☐

Pampering: Manicure ☐ Pedicure ☐ Facial ☐ Hairstyling ☐

Reading: Novels ☐ Magazines ☐ Blogs ☐ Comics ☐

Culture: Museum ☐ Theatre ☐ Concert ☐ Gallery ☐

Exercise: Swimming ☐ Running ☐ Yoga ☐ Aerobics ☐

TV: Cartoons ☐ Soaps ☐ Sitcoms ☐ Documentaries ☐

Day trip: Zoo ☐ Aquarium ☐ Water park ☐ Theme park ☐

Getting around: Bike ☐ Skateboard ☐ Walk ☐ Scooter ☐

At the beach: Snorkel ☐ Surf ☐ Sunbathe ☐ Sand castles ☐

YOUR INFLUENCES CLOCK

THINK ABOUT THE PEOPLE WHO'VE HAD AN IMPACT ON YOU DURING YOUR LIFE SO FAR. THEY COULD BE YOUR PARENTS, FRIENDS OR YOUR FAVOURITE CELEBS. WRITE THEIR NAMES IN THE TWELVE SPACES AROUND THE EDGE OF THE CLOCK, AND DRAW A PICTURE OF YOUR FACE IN THE MIDDLE.

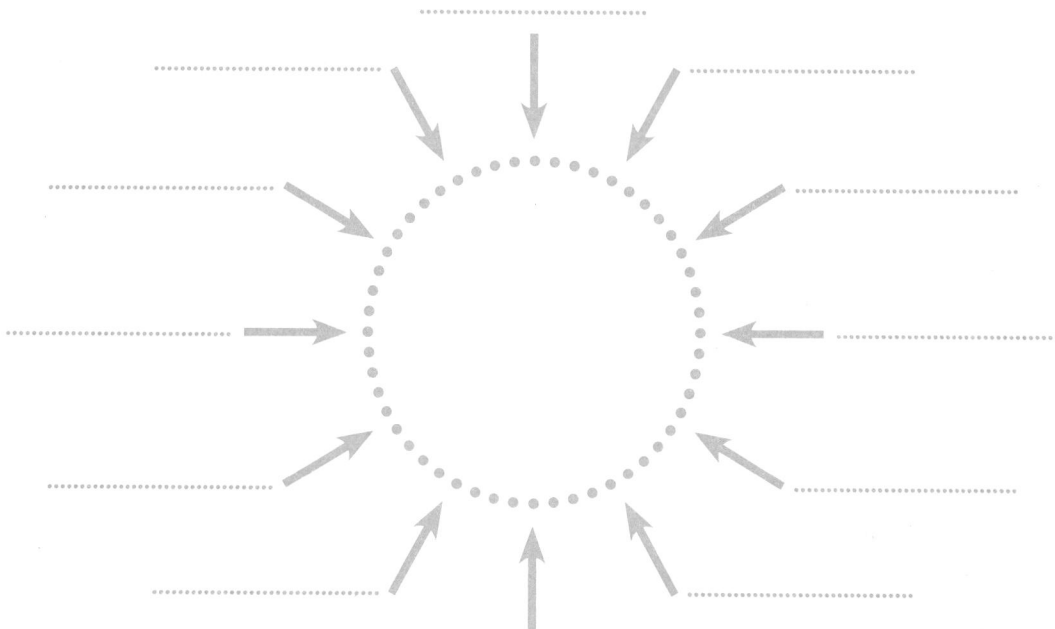

Date ....

Time .... Place ....

BEST BOOKS
OF ALL TIME

ORGANIZE THE BOOKS THAT YOU LIKE MOST INTO A LIST,
ACCORDING TO HOW MUCH YOU ENJOYED THEM AND HOW
MEMORABLE THEY ARE, WITH THE TITLE OF THE BOOK
THAT YOU THINK IS BEST AT NUMBER ONE.

Date .... Time .... Place ....

1. ....
2. ....
3. ....
4. ....
5. ....
6. ....
7. ....
8. ....

THE FILM OF YOUR LIFE ...

YOU'RE SUCH AN INCREDIBLE GIRL THAT SOMEONE IS SURE TO WANT TO MAKE A FILM ABOUT YOUR LIFE ONE DAY. OBVIOUSLY YOU'LL GET THE FINAL CASTING CHOICE, SO WHO WOULD YOU CHOOSE TO PLAY YOU, YOUR FAMILY AND YOUR FRIENDS?

Write the name of each 'character' you would want in the film in the column on the left, then which actor you think should play the part in the column on the right.

Date .... Time .... Place ....

ROLE	PLAYED BY

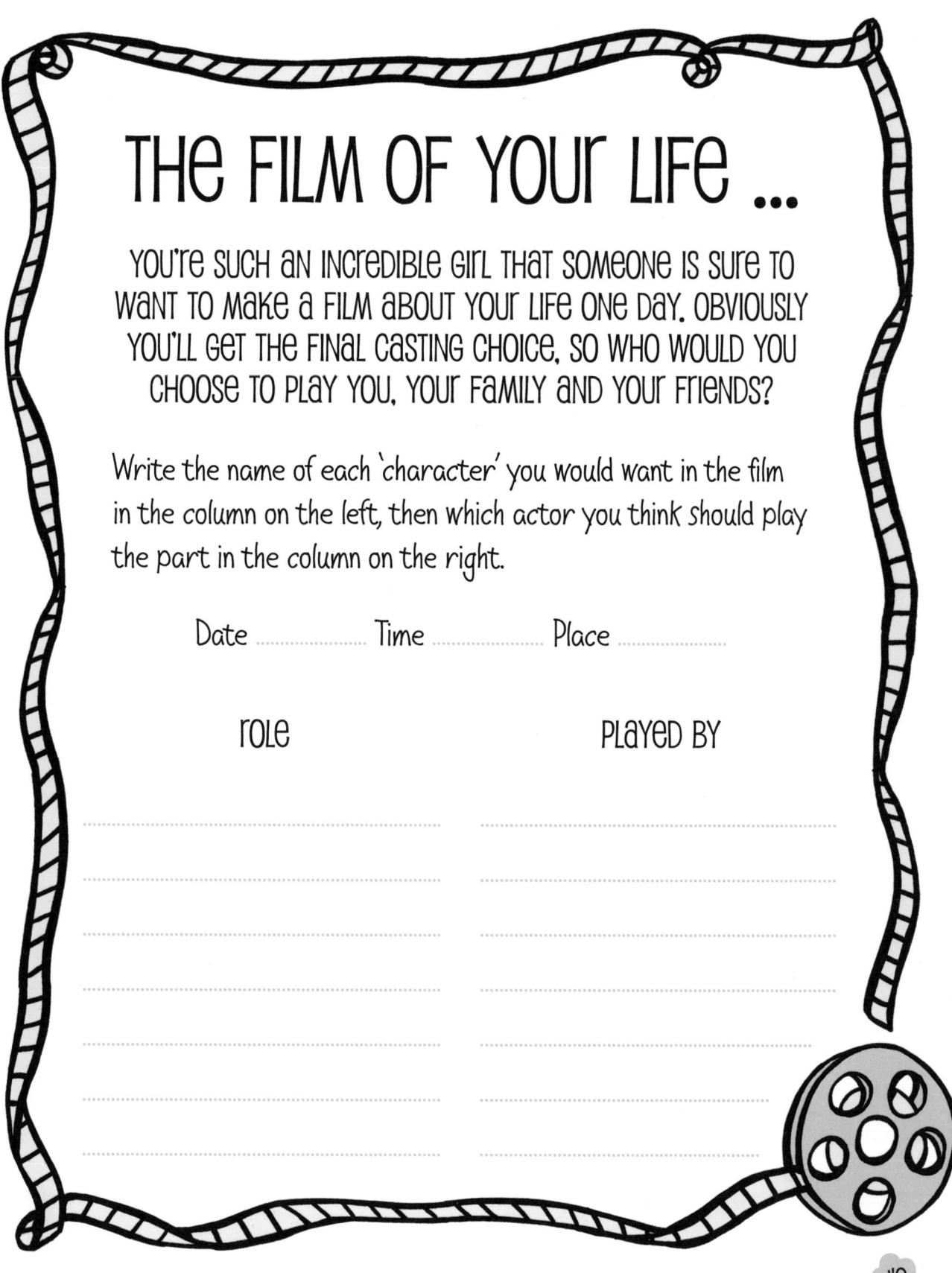

scariest
THINGS OF ALL TIME

everyone's fears are different, so the things that make your best friend squirm, scream or shudder, might be no sweat to you. take a deep breath, grab a pen and get ticking – it's time to face your fears. read each of the chilling choices on the opposite page, then tick the five of them that you're most afraid of.

Date .... Time .... Place ....

Slimy things ☐ Crawly things ☐

Spiky things ☐ Sticky things ☐

Science tests ☐ Maths tests ☐

History tests ☐ French tests ☐

Bungee jumping ☐ Scuba diving ☐

Sky-diving ☐ Whitewater rafting ☐

Spiders ☐ Bats ☐ Snakes ☐ Rats ☐

Lions ☐ Sharks ☐ Bears ☐ Wolves ☐

Singing on stage ☐ Making a speech in public ☐

Falling over at a disco ☐ No one knowing who you are ☐

Graveyards ☐ Caves ☐ Cellars ☐ Attics ☐

Ghosts ☐ Vampires ☐ Zombies ☐ Werewolves ☐

Roller coasters ☐ Lifts ☐ Fast cars ☐ Aeroplanes ☐

Travel Tales

FILL IN THIS PAGE WITH DETAILS OF YOUR MOST TERRIFIC TRIPS.

Date .... Time .... Place ....

Have you ever travelled overnight to get somewhere?

Yes ☐ No ☐

If 'yes', where to? ....

Ever been on a ferry ☐ a submarine ☐ a helicopter ☐
a bullet train ☐ a plane ☐ a pedalo ☐ a unicycle ☐ ?

Where was the last place you went on holiday?

....

Would you go there again? Yes ☐ No ☐

If 'no', why not? ....

Which destination is the furthest you have
ever travelled to?

....

ULTIMATE DESTINATION

USE THE CHART BELOW TO DISCOVER YOUR TRUE DREAM DESTINATION.

Date .... Time .... Place ....

Think of four places that you'd really like to go to and write them into
the cases on the top row of the chart. Decide which of each pair you
would want to visit most, and write them in the spaces on the second
row. Now, select the place you would want to visit more than the other.
This is your ultimate destination.

MISS THIS

THINK OF TEN THINGS YOU MISS WHEN YOU'RE AWAY FROM HOME. WRITE YOUR TOP TEN BELOW, WITH THE THING YOU MISS MOST AT NUMBER ONE.

1. ....
2. ....
3. ....
4. ....
5. ....
6. ....
7. ....
8. ....
9. ....
10. ....

Date .... Time ....

Place ....

DON'T MISS THAT

THINK OF TEN THINGS THAT YOU'RE GLAD TO GET AWAY FROM WHEN YOU'RE AWAY FROM HOME. WRITE YOUR TOP TEN BELOW, WITH THE THING YOU MISS LEAST AT NUMBER ONE.

1.
2.
3.
4.
5.
6.
7.
8.
9.
10.

Date   Time   Place

55

Forever
FOODS

IF YOU COULD EAT ONLY ONE ITEM FROM EACH LIST OF OPTIONS ON THE NEXT PAGE FOR THE REST OF YOUR LIFE, WHICH WOULD IT BE? TICK ONE ON EACH LINE.

Date .... Time .... Place ....

Breakfast: Toast ☐ Cereal ☐ Sausages ☐ Egg and beans ☐

Snacks: Chocolate ☐ Cakes ☐ Sweets ☐ Biscuits ☐

Popcorn: Sweet ☐ Salty ☐ Toffee ☐ Plain ☐

Crisps: Plain ☐ Bacon ☐ Prawn cocktail ☐ Cheese ☐

Vegetables: Carrots ☐ Broccoli ☐ Peas ☐ Cabbage ☐

Ice cream: Chocolate ☐ Strawberry ☐ Vanilla ☐ Mint ☐

Fruit: Oranges ☐ Bananas ☐ Grapes ☐ Apples ☐

Scary: Snails ☐ Frogs' legs ☐ Jellied eels ☐ Fried insects ☐

Draw your favourite meal of all time on the plate below.

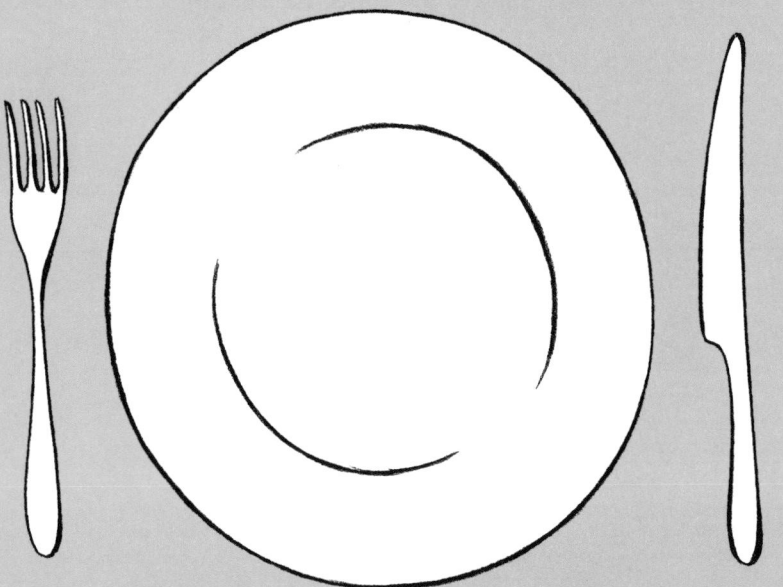

are you a daredevil?

Date .... Time .... Place ....

TICK a, B, or C TO aNSWer THESE DareDevIL QUESTIONS.
THEN, COUNT UP HOW MANY OF EACH YOU HAVE SELECTED
AND LOOK ON PAGE 59 FOR THE RESULTS.

WOULD YOU ever ...

	A I'm in!	B Maybe	C No way!
... do a sky-dive?	☐	☐	☐
... swim with sharks?	☐	☐	☐
... hold a tarantula?	☐	☐	☐
... go upside down on a fair ride?	☐	☐	☐
... stay in a haunted house?	☐	☐	☐
... ride a motorbike?	☐	☐	☐
... do a bungee jump?	☐	☐	☐
... fly a plane?	☐	☐	☐
... walk a tightrope?	☐	☐	☐
... go whitewater rafting?	☐	☐	☐

Daring answers

Mostly 'A's: Fearless fanatic

You are the ultimate daredevil! Always up for a new challenge, you never turn down a dare. This sometimes worries people and forces them to put rules in place that stop you taking things too far.

Mostly 'B's: Balanced babe

You're a brave lady who's not afraid to try new things, but you always weigh up the pros and cons first. You think carefully before taking the plunge, and people give you lots of freedom because they know they can trust you to make the right decision.

Mostly 'C's: Safe sister

You're a cautious girl who likes to play it safe. You hate being put into risky situations, and are always the first to stop your friends getting into trouble. People respect this, but also encourage you not to be afraid to try new things.

TOP TEN PEOPLE
YOU ADMIRE

THINK OF TEN PEOPLE THAT YOU REALLY ADMIRE,
THEN ORGANIZE THEM INTO A TOP TEN, ACCORDING
TO HOW IMPORTANT THEY ARE TO YOU.

Date .... Time .... Place ....

Your favourite should be number one. Write a name by each
number, then say why you admire them on the line underneath.

1. ....

....

2. ....

....

3. ....

....

4. ....

....

5. ....

....

6. ....

....

7. ....

....

8. ....

....

9. ....

....

10. ....

....

Family Fortunes

Ask seven family members or close friends to make a wish for you and write it in the fortune cookie papers below. Remember to check back to see if their wishes for you come true.

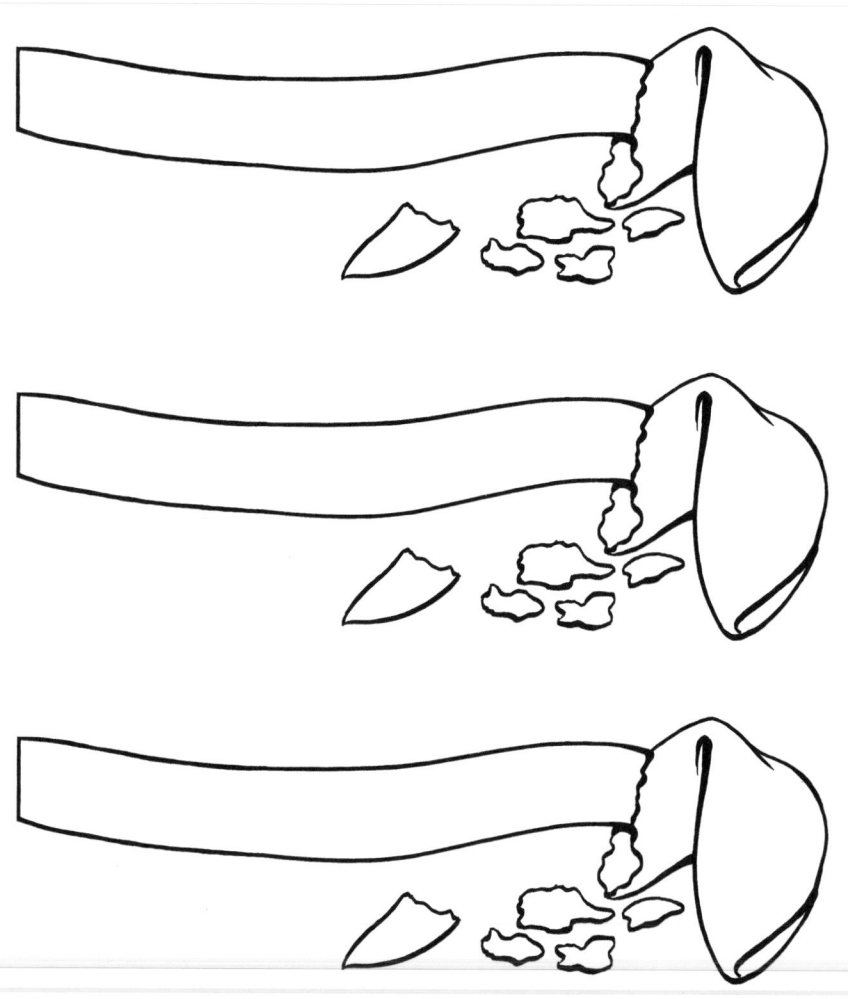

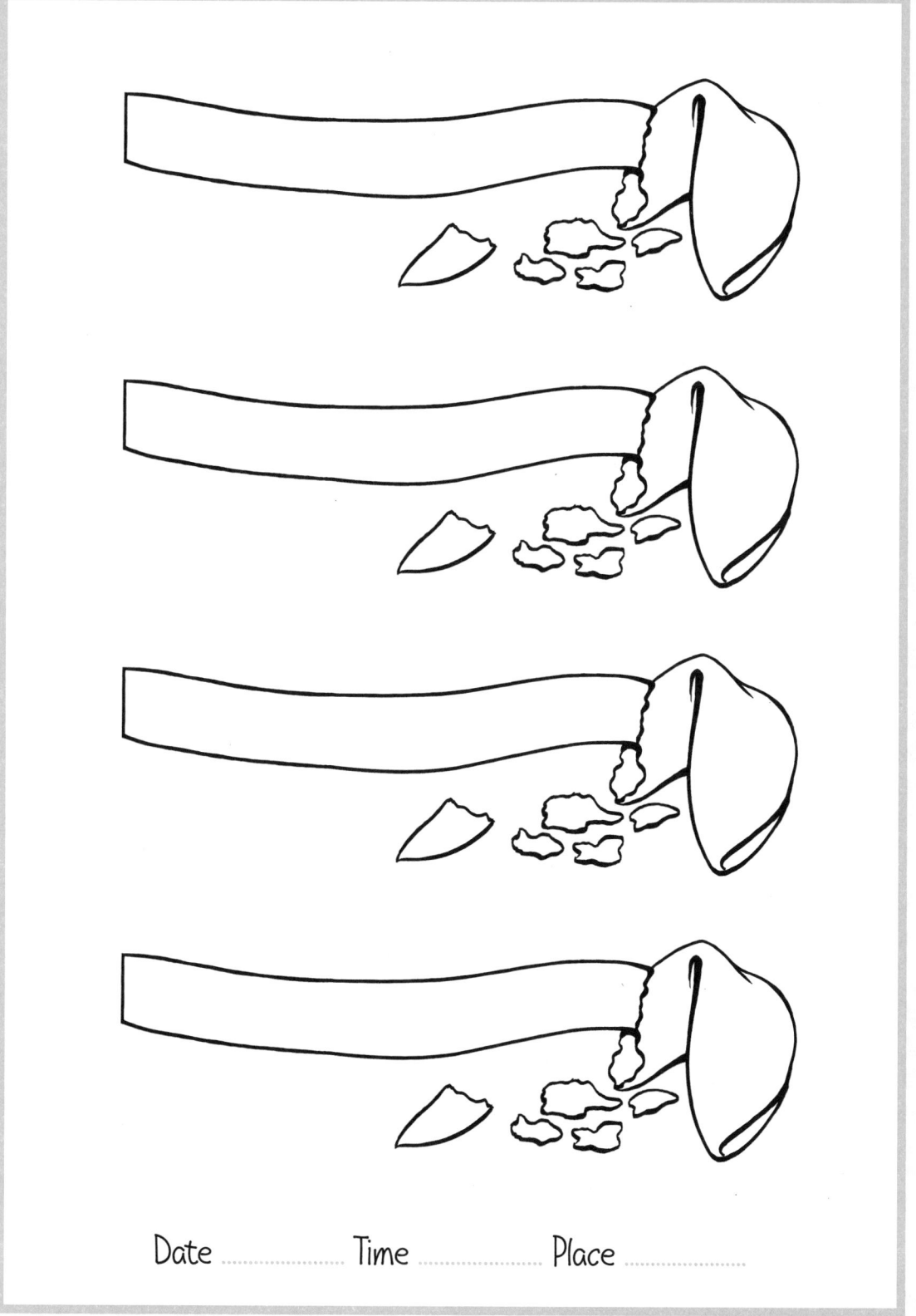

Date .... Time .... Place ....

IN-DEPTH INTERVIEW

HAVE YOU EVER WANTED TO KNOW MORE ABOUT ONE OF YOUR FAVOURITE RELATIVES? THIS IS YOUR CHANCE.

Date .... Time .... Place ....

You might pick a grandparent, or an aunt or uncle, but choose a relation that you'd like to get to know better. Put these questions to them in an interview. If there is anything you have been dying to ask, now is the time. At the end of the list of questions, there is space to add your own 'burning question', ready to ask your subject.

What is your full name?

....

When and where were you born?

....

Where did you grow up?

....

How are we related?

....

What is your earliest memory?

....

....

What's your earliest memory of me?

....

....

What did you want to be when you grew up?

....

....

What did you actually do?

....

....

What is your proudest achievement?

....

....

What is your favourite place in the whole world, and why?

....

....

What did you like most about school?

....

Who was your best friend when you were my age?

....

Which person did you most admire when you were my age?

....

Why? ....

....

What is the most important news event

that has happened in your lifetime?

....

....

....

What is the best present you have ever been given?

....

....

If you had one piece of advice to give me,

what would it be?

....

....

What is your most treasured possession?

....

....

My burning question is:

....

....

The answer is:

....

....

Personal
Profiler

answer these questions, and make a note of how many times you answer a, b, c or d, then turn to page 71 to discover the secrets of your personality.

Date .... Time .... Place ....

What do you love most about your best friend?

a. You never know what she's going to do next
b. She's always first to know when there's a party
c. She totally understands you
d. You can rely on her to be there for you always

Your friend calls you in tears. What do you do?

a. Listen carefully and try to help her see that it's not so bad
b. Arrange an outing to take her mind off the problem
c. Head straight to her house with a tub of ice cream
d. Offer some practical solutions to the problem

Which do you find most annoying?

a. Being made to follow lots of rules
b. Being grounded
c. Being lied to
d. Being rushed into a quick decision

A friend comes round to ask you to the park. What do you do?

a. Immediately go with her
b. Call for other people on the way
c. Invite her in for a drink and a chat first
d. Ask her to wait while you grab a few things you'll need

During lunch break, where can you usually be found?

a. Painting in the art room
b. Hanging out in a big group
c. Having an intense chat with your best friend
d. Flicking through magazines

What do you prefer to watch on TV?

a. You don't really watch much TV
b. Music programmes
c. Soap operas with characters you can really relate to
d. Documentaries about amazing animals and beautiful places

What's your bedroom like?

a. Full of colour
b. A bit of a mess with loads of photos of friends on the walls
c. Peaceful - a tranquil retreat
d. Everything's in exactly the right place, it's perfectly organized

Your friend is off to a party and asks you to do her hair. What do you do?

a. Create an amazing new style
b. Let her choose from all the latest styles in magazines
c. Do it exactly the way she wants
d. Use straighteners, tongs and lots of products to create a sensational style.

Your Personal Profile Answers

Mostly 'A's: Bohemian babe

Unconventional and imaginative, you're a true free spirit. Your spontaneous nature means that life's never dull when you're around. You think with your heart and always follow your instincts.

Mostly 'B's: Social butterfly

Warm-hearted and easy-going, you have loads of friends and are always the life and soul of the party. You're super-confident but don't forget to take some time out to unwind every now and again.

Mostly 'C's: Caring and kind

A great friend, you're always there for people when they need you. You build strong, deep relationships and prefer to spend time with people you love and trust.

Mostly 'D's: Smart cookie.

A bright spark, you're highly intelligent and a quick thinker. You're practical, logical and can take care of yourself in any situation. People admire your down-to-earth approach to life.

BEST GAMES OF ALL TIME

COMPILE A LIST OF YOUR TOP-TEN FAVOURITE GAMES, IN ORDER OF HOW MUCH YOU LIKE THEM.

Date .... Time .... Place ....

They might be computer games, playground games or even games you've invented with your friends. Make sure that your favourite game goes at number one.

1. ....
2. ....
3. ....
4. ....
5. ....
6. ....
7. ....
8. ....
9. ....
10. ....

FOUR SEASONS IN ONE PAGE

IN THE SPACES BELOW, USE WORDS OR PICTURES TO DESCRIBE
THE THINGS YOU LIKE BEST ABOUT EACH OF THE SEASONS.

Date .... Time .... Place ....

Think about the weather, the kinds of clothes you wear, the activities
you do and any celebrations that take place at that time of year.

SPRING

SUMMER

AUTUMN

WINTER

SUPERPOWER SHOWDOWN

THINK OF FOUR SUPERPOWERS THAT YOU WOULD MOST LIKE TO HAVE – THESE COULD BE ANYTHING FROM BEING INVISIBLE TO BEING ABLE TO STOP TIME.

Date .... Time .... Place ....

Write one in each space on the first row. Then, choose which superpower from each pair you would most like to have. Write it in the space below. Lastly, decide which of the final two is the ultimate superpower you would like to have, and write it in the final space.

YOUR SUPERHERO COSTUME

THE GREATEST SUPERHEROES ALWAYS HAVE A SUPER-STYLISH OUTFIT SO THAT THEY STAND OUT FROM THE CROWD.

Date .... Time .... Place ....

Design a spectacular costume of your own in the space on the right. What would your superhero name be? Fill it in below.

BODY TRICKS

TICK OFF EACH THING THAT YOU
AND YOUR FRIENDS CAN DO.

Date ....
Time ....
Place ....

Fill out each person's name in the spaces along the top.

Roll your tongue into a tube

Wiggle your ears

Raise one eyebrow

Touch your nose with your tongue

Lick your elbow

Twitch your nose

Is there anything else you can do that none of your friends can?

Yes ☐ No ☐

If 'yes', describe what it is here:

....

....

GUILTY PLEASURES

THINK OF THINGS YOU KNOW YOU SHOULDN'T
LIKE, YET YOU CAN'T HELP BUT LOVE.

Date .... Time .... Place ....

Perhaps there's a cheesy song that isn't cool but always gets you dancing. Or maybe a toy that's for little kids you still like to play with! Write four of these things in the first row, then put which from each pair you enjoy most in the second row. Out of the final two, you must decide which is your ultimate guilty pleasure.

PET PROFILE

COMPLETE THE INFORMATION BELOW, EITHER ABOUT YOUR FAVOURITE PET OR A DREAM PET THAT YOU'D LOVE TO OWN.

Name .... Age ....

Type of animal ....

Boy ☐ Girl ☐ Colour ....

Likes ....

Dislikes ....

What's the funniest thing your pet does?

....

What's the naughtiest thing your pet does?

....

Date .... Time .... Place ....

FINGERPRINT FUN

Take your prints

Draw around your hand in the space opposite. Then dip the top of each of your fingers in some paint, or an ink pad. Carefully press each fingertip on to the corresponding finger on the page to record your fingerprints.

Did you know?

Most people say that each human fingerprint is unique, but this isn't necessarily true. The only way you'd know for certain is to check the fingerprints of everyone who has ever lived! In fact, different people's fingerprints can sometimes be similar enough even to fool experts, leading to several cases of mistaken identity.

Your fingernails (and toenails for that matter) are made from the same stuff as your hair - 'keratin'. This is a protein that is also found in birds' feathers and animals' hooves.

If you stopped moving your hand for a long enough time, the lines on your palms and fingers would eventually smooth out.

WHY NOT DOODLE SOME HENNA PATTERNS ON YOUR
HAND ONCE YOU'VE FINISHED YOUR FINGERPRINTS?

DRAW AROUND YOUR HAND IN THIS BOX.

Date .... Time .... Place ....

Party Planner

JUST IMAGINE YOU'RE AN EVENTS ORGANIZER WHO'S BEEN GIVEN AN UNLIMITED BUDGET TO PUT TOGETHER THE WORLD'S GREATEST EVER PARTY.

Date   Time   Place

Firstly, what would your party be celebrating?

....

....

All the best parties have a theme, whether it's the colour of outfits people can wear, or a particular subject for fancy dress - what would yours be?

....

....

If you could ask any band, pop star, or DJ to provide the music, who would it be?

....

....

Would there be any other entertainment? Yes ☐ No ☐

If 'yes', what would it be?

....

....

....

What kind of food and drink would you choose?

....

....

....

What would you wear?

....

....

....

What decorations would you choose for your party?

....

....

If you could ask anyone in the world to go with you to the party, who would it be?

....

BEST MOMENTS
OF ALL TIME

THINK OF THE BEST THINGS THAT HAVE EVER HAPPENED TO YOU (SO FAR) – PERHAPS WHEN A BABY BROTHER OR SISTER WAS BORN, OR THE FEELING YOU GOT THE FIRST TIME YOU RODE A BIKE WITHOUT HELP. ONCE YOU'VE THOUGHT OF YOUR FIVE BEST MOMENTS, LIST THEM IN ORDER SO THAT YOUR ALL-TIME FAVOURITE IS AT NUMBER ONE.

1. ....

....

2. ....

....

3. ....

....

4. ....

....

5. ....

....

Date .... Time .... Place ....

BEST FRIENDS Forever?

HOW WELL DO YOU AND YOUR FRIENDS KNOW EACH OTHER?

Date .... Time ....

Place ....

Read through the questions opposite and fill in your answers. (Copy out the questions for your friends to fill in, too.) Then quiz your friends to find out just how well they know you. Make a note of the number of questions they each get right. Turn the page for the results.

1. What date is my birthday?

....

2. What is my favourite colour?

....

3. Who is my celebrity crush?

....

4. What is my favourite animal?

....

5. What is my favourite food?

....

6. What do I want to be when I grow up?

....

7. What is my most embarrassing moment, so far?

....

8. What is my all-time favourite film?

....

9. What is my all-time favourite book?

....

10. Where in the world would I most like to visit?

....

THE SCORES

0-3. Oops! Looks like you need to spend a little more quality time together and get to know each other better.

4-7. You are certainly good friends, but you've still got some sharing to do before you become truly best buddies.

8-10. Wow. You're as close as sisters and have no secrets from each other – you can always rely on one another in a crisis.

AGONY-AUNT CHALLENGE

AGONY AUNTS (AND UNCLES) OFTEN WORK FOR NEWSPAPERS AND MAGAZINES. THEY HELP WITH PROBLEMS THAT READERS SEND IN BY OFFERING THEIR ADVICE.

Why not get together with a group of friends and choose a problem to respond to? Discuss the advice you could give if someone asked your opinion. Practise your own agony-aunt skills by chatting together and each providing an answer to one of the problems on the next page. Fill in your name in the spaces provided.

Date ....
Time ....
Place ....

'Dear Auntie ....

A new girl has started at my school and my best friend has been spending loads of time with her. I'm feeling really left out and keep arguing with my best friend. What should I do?'

'Dear Auntie ....

My sister is so annoying! She is a massive show-off and gets all the attention. She is younger than me and whenever she does something wrong I get the blame. Help!'

'Dear Auntie ....

I'm finding it difficult to fit in everything I want to do at the moment. We're getting tons of homework and I go to lots of after-school clubs. I don't want to give them up, but my marks are quite bad. Do you have any ideas?'

'Dear Auntie

I feel like I'm always being compared to my older sister.
She's really clever and always gets top marks at school. She's
also popular and has lots of friends. How can I deal with the
pressure to do as well as her?'

WHAT'S YOUR PROBLEM?

With your friends, think of three problems you would like to ask
an agony aunt about. Put them in order, with the most important
problem at number one. See if you and your friends can come up
with any solutions yourselves, or ask a parent for advice.

1. ....

....

2. ....

....

3. ....

....

SIGN OF
THE TIMES

ask each of your best friends to sign their name in the space below for you to look back at in the future.

Date .... Time .... Place ....

SURVIVAL SKILLS

IF YOU WERE MAROONED ON A DESERT ISLAND, BUT WITHOUT ANY ESSENTIAL ITEMS, WHICH OF THE FOLLOWING CHALLENGES WOULD YOU BE WILLING TO ATTEMPT WHILE WAITING TO BE RESCUED? TURN TO PAGE 94 TO FIND OUT YOUR SKILL RATING.

Date .... Time .... Place ....

	A Absolutely	B Maybe	C No way!
Build a fire	☐	☐	☐
Catch a fish	☐	☐	☐
Dig a well	☐	☐	☐
Make a raft	☐	☐	☐
Build a shelter	☐	☐	☐
Make an animal trap	☐	☐	☐
Escape from quicksand	☐	☐	☐
Make a bow and arrow	☐	☐	☐
Use leaves as toilet roll	☐	☐	☐
Eat bugs	☐	☐	☐

survival answers

Mostly 'A's: Super survivor

Your survival skills are top notch and you love the great outdoors. You feel as at home in a forest as most people would in a five-star hotel! You could take care of yourself for weeks on end, if ever you found yourself stranded.

Mostly 'B's: Adventurous amiga

You haven't had the opportunity to practise many survival skills, but you're an adventurous girl who would love to give it a go! You don't mind getting your hands dirty (or eating the odd bug for survival).

Mostly 'C's: Indoor individual

Outdoor living is not for you, and you wouldn't last long if you were marooned on your own. You're accustomed to the finer things in life and even the thought of camping makes your blood run cold!

BOYS - FRIENDS OR FOES?

ask your friends to suggest ten famous boys for you. write each name in one of the spaces below. think about each boy and decide whether you would be friends or foes. 'undecided' is not an option!

Date   Time   Place

                                    FRIEND   FOE

WOULD YOU rather?

STUDY EACH OF THE CHEEKY CHOICES BELOW AND DECIDE
WHICH YOU WOULD rATHER CHOOSE IF YOU REALLY HAD TO.

Date .... Time .... Place ....

Have no eyebrows ☐
Have eyebrows that meet in the middle ☐

Never wash your hair again ☐
Never wash your pants again ☐

Be popular but ugly ☐ Be beautiful but unpopular ☐

Have no TV ☐ Have a TV that only showed adverts ☐

Never listen to any music again ☐
Always listen to classical music ☐

Spend a night in a haunted house ☐
Spend a night on your own in the woods ☐

Have hiccups for a month ☐
Do nothing but maths for a whole day ☐

Be able to paint your nails just by looking at them ☐
Be able to style your hair just by thinking about it ☐

Burp every time a boy talks to you ☐
Fart every time a girl talks to you ☐

Go to school in just your underwear for a day ☐
Go to school in a clown outfit for one month ☐

Find a secret treasure stash ☐
Make a new friend ☐

HEADLINE NEWS

HAVE YOU NOTICED WHAT'S GOING ON IN THE NEWS LATELY?

Date .... Time .... Place ....

What do you think are the five most important news stories at the moment? Make a list and write them in order so that the one that you think is most memorable is at number one.

1. ....
2. ....
3. ....
4. ....
5. ....

HEADLINE-MAKER

WHAT ARE THE FIVE MOST IMPORTANT THINGS THAT HAPPENED TO YOU THIS WEEK?

Date .... Time .... Place ....

Make a list of these events, so that the most important event is at number one.

1. ....
2. ....
3. ....
4. ....
5. ....

FRIENDSHIP GALLERY

GET FOUR FRIENDS TO EACH DRAW A PORTRAIT OF YOU IN ONE OF THESE FRAMES AND SIGN THEIR MASTERPIECE UNDERNEATH. THEN, IN THE FRAME AT THE BOTTOM OF PAGE 101, ASK THEM TO EACH WRITE ONE WORD THAT THEY THINK BEST DESCRIBES YOU.

Date .... Time .... Place ....

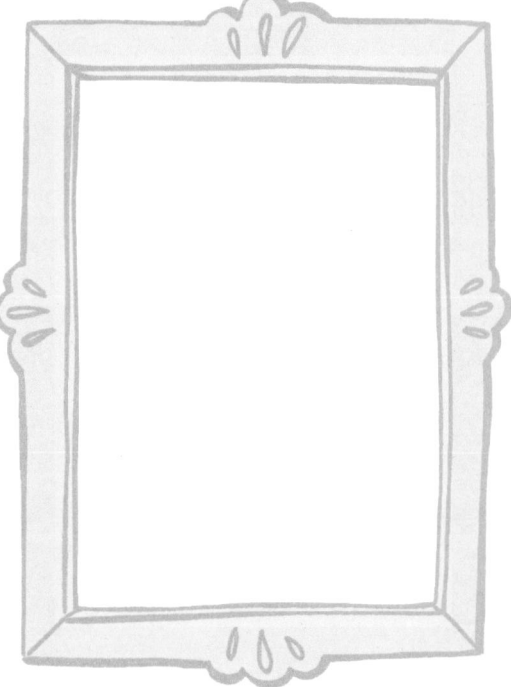

Signed .... Signed ....

Signed .... Signed ....

TV ADDICT

THINK OF YOUR TEN FAVOURITE TELEVISION PROGRAMMES, THEN ORGANIZE YOUR LIST INTO A TOP TEN, ACCORDING TO HOW MUCH YOU REALLY ENJOY THEM. YOUR FAVOURITE SHOULD BE AT NUMBER ONE.

Date   Time   Place

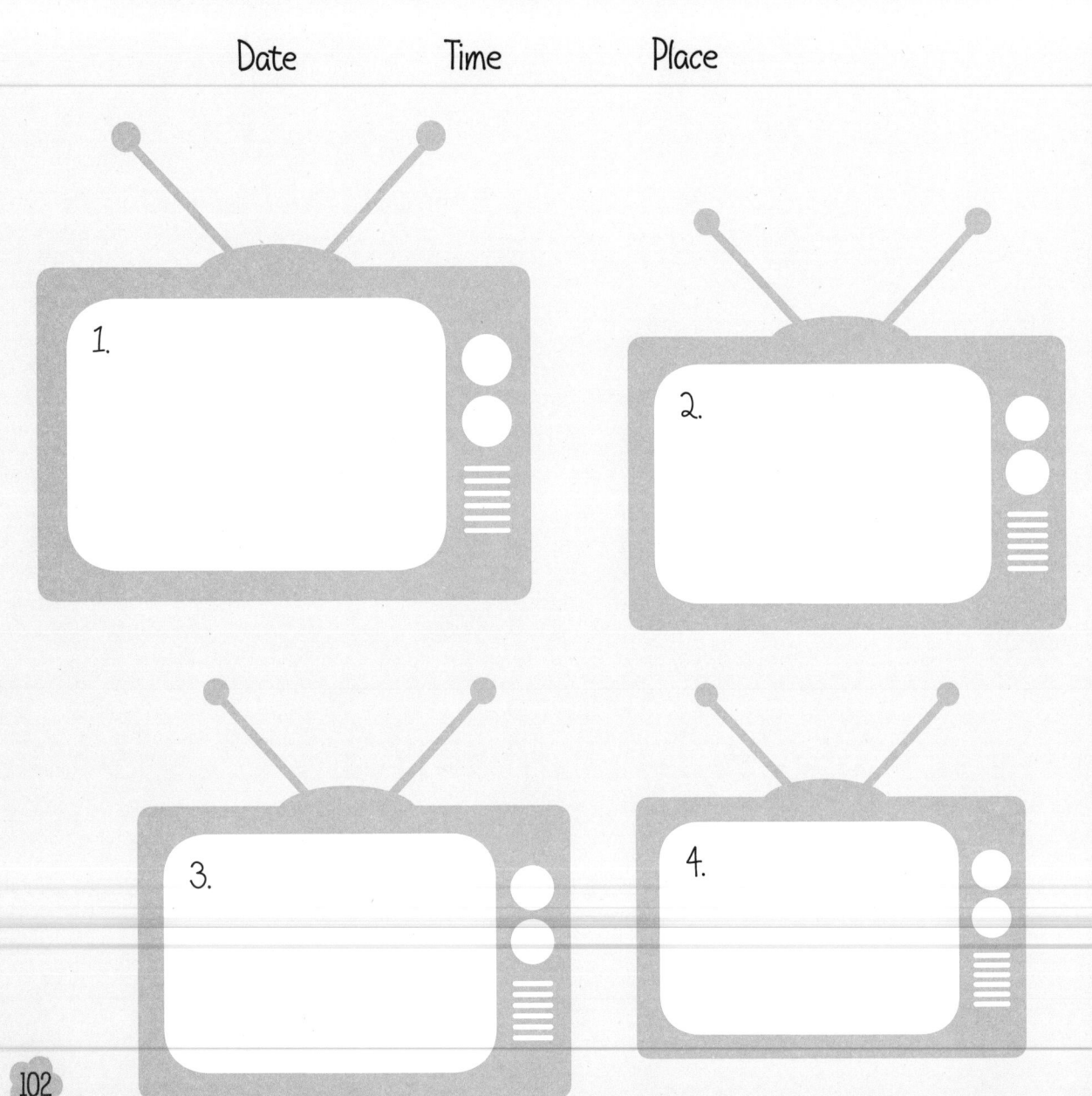

1.

2.

3.

4.

5.

6.

7.

8.

9.

10.

WHAT DO YOUR DOODLES DO?

THE WAY YOU WRITE AND DRAW CAN REVEAL A LOT ABOUT YOUR PERSONALITY. MAKE YOUR MARK ON THE FOLLOWING PAGES THEN TURN TO PAGES 108 TO 110 TO DISCOVER WHAT YOUR DOODLING STYLE MEANS.

Date .... Time .... Place ....

First, don't think about it too much, but just sign your name in the box below:

TIME TO WRITE

Now copy out the words, 'This is what my writing looks like,' below:

Now, turn the page and get doodling ...

Join the ends of this line, any way you like:

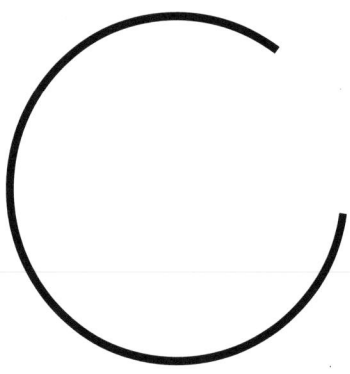

DO A DOODLE

Use this space to doodle the first thing that comes into your head.

Now copy this spiral in the space on the right.

PIG PEN

Lastly, draw a picture of a pig here.

Now turn the page to find out what your writing and doodles say about you.

signature style

If your signature is large and fills the box, you're an outgoing girl who loves to be the centre of attention.

Ellen Bailey

If your signature's small and there's lots of space around it you're a thoughtful girl who enjoys spending time on her own.

Ellen Bailey

time to write

If your writing leans to the right '*like this*', you're warm, caring and emotional. Your heart rules your head.

If your writing stands upright 'like this', you're good at keeping your emotions in check and have a balanced attitude.

If your writing leans to the left 'like this', you try to conceal your feelings from others. Your head rules your heart.

CIRCLE OF TRUTH

If you completed the circle like this, you're a conventional girl who values traditions. You're practical, sensible and trustworthy.

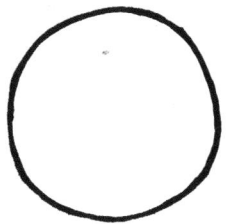

If you completed the circle with zigzag lines, you have a strong sense of responsibility but also like to take the occasional risk.

If you turned the circle into something else completely, you're an imaginative, creative girl who hates being made to follow rules.

DO a DOODLE

Hearts and flowers: You're all about peace and love. You're caring, kind and thoughtful.

Geometric shapes: You're a clear thinker - organized and good at planning.

Patterns: You have lots of energy and are always on the go. You're creative and good at paying attention to detail.

People and animals: You're a warm, friendly girl with a big heart. You dislike spending time on your own.

 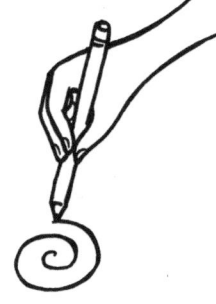

If you started at the outside of the spiral and drew inwards, you like to look at the big picture and think about the details afterwards.

If you started at the inside of the spiral and drew outwards, you like to focus on details before thinking about how they fit into the bigger plan.

PIG PEN

If the pig is facing to the left, you spend a lot of time thinking about the past. You have an excellent memory.

If the pig is facing forwards, you live in the present and appreciate each moment as it happens.

If the pig is facing to the right, you are always busy thinking about the future and what's going to happen next.

BEST NAMES EVER

LIST YOUR TEN FAVOURITE GIRLS' NAMES AND YOUR TEN FAVOURITE BOYS' NAMES. ORGANIZE EACH LIST INTO A TOP TEN, ACCORDING TO HOW MUCH YOU LOVE THEM, SO THAT YOUR FAVOURITES ARE AT NUMBER ONE.

Date .... Time .... Place ....

GIRLS' NAMES

1. ....
2. ....
3. ....
4. ....
5. ....
6. ....
7. ....
8. ....
9. ....
10. ....

BOYS' NAMES

1. ....
2. ....
3. ....
4. ....
5. ....
6. ....
7. ....
8. ....
9. ....
10. ....

are you a MONEY MASTER?

MAKE A NOTE OF THE NUMBER OF TIMES YOU ANSWER a, b, or c IN THIS QUIZ, THEN TURN TO PAGE 115 TO DISCOVER IF YOU CONTROL YOUR MONEY OR IF YOUR MONEY CONTROLS YOU!

It's your best friend's birthday next week and you haven't bought her a present yet. Which would you decide to do?

a. Buy her the expensive shoes she's been wanting for months
b. Make her something instead of buying it – home-made gifts show that you care, and you can make it more personal, too
c. Club together with some friends to buy her the shoes she loves from all of you

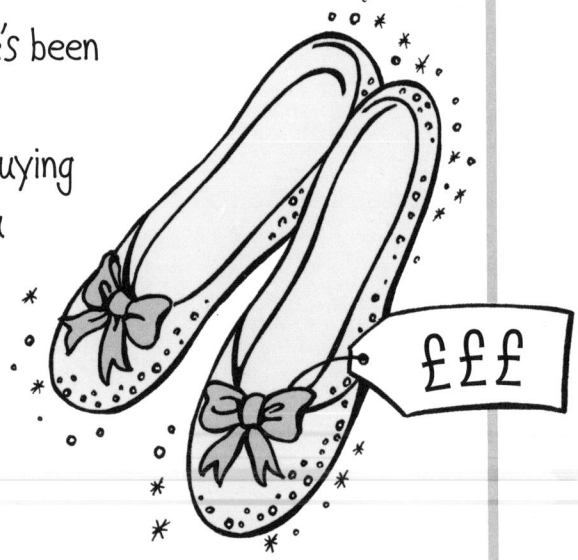

£££

You see a great dress for the school dance in a shop window. Which would you decide to do?

a. Go right in and buy it without even trying it on
b. Look at the price tag before you do anything else
c. Try it on, and make sure you can think of at least three different occasions on which you can wear it before you buy it

It's time to plan a family holiday. Would you:

a. Start thumbing through glossy holiday brochures?
b. Dig out your tent and get ready for some camping fun?
c. Research online and shop around for the best deals?

The latest issue of your favourite magazine is out. Would you:

a. Buy it straightaway? It's got all the gossip on your favourite celebrities and you don't want to miss out
b. Leave it on the shelves? You've been saving for ages, and you're sure you can find out the gossip from your friends anyway
c. Go halves with your best friend? You can read it together and have fun sharing the stories

Congratulations! You've won £50 in a competition. Will you:

a. Hit the shops the first chance you get?
b. Put it in the bank? It's sure to come in handy in the future
c. Save some of it, but treat yourself to something new as well?

You can't decide which of two bags to buy. Are you more likely to:

a. Buy them both - they'll both get used?
b. Buy the cheapest one?
c. Buy the one that goes with more of your outfits?

Your friends are planning a cinema trip. You really want to go, but can't afford it. Would you:

a. Borrow the money from your parents and go anyway? You'll just have to do more chores than usual to make up for it
b. Tell your friends you can't make it and have an evening in?
c. Invite everyone round for a DVD party at your house instead?

Date .... Time .... Place ....

Money-Master answers

Mostly 'A's: Shopaholic.

You really love to shop! However, learning to save
money rather than splashing out is a useful skill.
Try to save a little each month, wait until your piggy
bank is bulging, then reward yourself by using it to
buy something really special.

Mostly 'B's: Supersaver.

Thoughtful and cautious, you are very
careful with your money and will rarely
buy anything unless you really need it.
It's important to spend wisely, but make
sure you remember to treat yourself to
something fun every once in a while.

Mostly 'C's: Money master.

You keep an eye on your cash and
make sure you don't spend too
much, yet you're still able to buy the
things you want by saving up for them.
Keep up the good work.

MUSIC MIXES

WHETHER YOU WANT TO CHEER YOURSELF UP, OR JUST WANT TO GET IN THE PARTY SPIRIT, MUSIC CAN HAVE AN AMAZING EFFECT ON YOUR MOOD. USE THIS SPACE TO LIST AND ORDER YOUR FAVOURITE SONGS OR PIECES OF MUSIC FOR EACH CATEGORY.

Date .... Time .... Place ....

RELAXING

1. ....
2. ....
3. ....
4. ....
5. ....

DANCE-TASTIC

1. ....
2. ....
3. ....
4. ....
5. ....

SAD AND SOULFUL

1. ....
2. ....
3. ....
4. ....
5. ....

OH-SO-ANNOYING

1. ....
2. ....
3. ....
4. ....
5. ....

FANTASY BAND ON TOUR

IT DOESN'T MATTER IF YOU DON'T PLAY AN INSTRUMENT, ANYONE CAN HAVE A SUCCESSFUL FANTASY BAND!

First, you need to choose your bandmates and decide which role everyone should take within your band. Assign each role below to the friend you think it suits most.

Lead singer ....

Lead guitarist ....

Bass guitarist ....

Drummer ....

Keyboards ....

Backing singer 1 ....

Backing singer 2 ....

Tour manager ....

recording stars

Next, it's time to give your band a name. Circle your favourite word from each column below. Add them together to complete the name of your band. You might consider writing them out in an unusual way - for example, as one word, such as 'Superblueflowers' - to make your fantasy band's name a bit different.

Party	Funk	Kittens
Cute	Soul	Flowers
Pretty	Green	Singers
Super	Pink	Seeds
Girly	Rock	Things
Crazy	Blue	Flyers

name that tune

Now choose the title of your first single, which will go straight to number one in the charts. If you're stuck, use the name of your band as inspiration. For example, if your band is called the 'Superpinkseeds', you might call your song, 'Growing Up Pink'.

First single ....

Weeks at number one

....

Design your show-stopping album cover in the space below.

Date .... Time .... Place ....

LOOKING FOR LOVE

ever wondered How you'll recognize your one true love when they come along? rank the personality qualities below from 1-5, where 1 is not important and 5 is really important, so you know exactly what you're looking for in the perfect partner.

	1	2	3	4	5
Funny					
Confident					
Intelligent					
Mature					
Cool					
Ambitious					
Enthusiastic					
Sensitive					
Easy-going					
Independent					

Date .... Time .... Place ....

FLOWER OF DESTINY

Have you ever wondered who you might be destined to go out with in the future? Work it out using the flower of destiny.

Date .... Time .... Place ....

1. First, write a different name in each of the flower petals on the opposite page. Each of these people could end up as your one true love, so think carefully about who you choose.

2. Count the number of letters in your first name, and add it to the number of letters in your surname.

3. Divide this number by two. If you end up with a half number round it up. (For example, if you get 5.5, round it up to 6).

4. Starting at the top petal, count round the flower petals until you reach your number; then colour in that petal.

5. Continue counting your way round, starting on the next uncoloured petal. Skip any that are already coloured in. Every time you reach your number, colour in that petal.

6. When there is only one petal left uncoloured, the flower has spoken! That person is the one you are destined to fall in love with.

BEST FILMS OF ALL TIME

CAN YOU DECIDE WHICH ARE THE TEN BEST FILMS YOU HAVE EVER SEEN? ONCE YOU'VE DECIDED WHAT THEY ARE, ORGANIZE YOUR LIST INTO A TOP TEN, ACCORDING TO HOW MUCH YOU ENJOY THEM, WITH THE VERY BEST FILM AT NUMBER ONE.

Date .... Time .... Place ....

1.

2.

3.

4.

5.

6.

7.

8.

9.

10.

IF I were ...

Date .... Time .... Place ....

Think about the kind of person you are, and the things that you like, then decide what you'd be in each of the categories below. For example, if you are an energetic, playful person, you might choose a Labrador puppy as the animal you'd be.

If I were an animal, I'd be a ....

If I were a drink, I'd be a ....

If I were a colour, I'd be ....

If I were a country, I'd be ....

If I were a shop, I'd be ....

If I were a pop star, I'd be ....

If I were a musical instrument, I'd be a ....

If I were an ice-cream flavour, I'd be ....

If I were a subject at school, I'd be ....

If I were a fairy-tale character, I'd be ....

If I were a sport, I'd be ....

TOP TEN THINGS
I LIKE ABOUT ME

ORGANIZE THE TEN THINGS YOU LIKE MOST ABOUT
YOURSELF INTO A TOP TEN, ACCORDING TO HOW YOU RATE
EACH POINT, WITH THE BEST AT NUMBER ONE.

Date .... Time .... Place ....

1. ....

2. ....

3. ....

4. ....

5. ....

6. ....

7. ....

8. ....

9. ....

10. ....

also available:

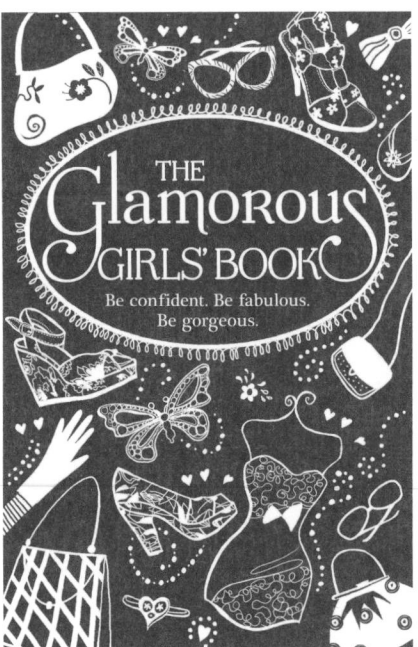

THE GLAMOROUS GIRLS' BOOK
978-1-78055-020-6

GIRLS' MISCELLANY
978-1-78055-041-1

THE GIRLS' SECRET HANDBOOK
978-1-78055-080-7